Quick'n'Easy

Yogurt, yoghurt or yoghourt ... however you spell it, or, for that matter, say it, yogurt is said to be "the food of the gods". Much has been written and researched about this wonderful food and ingredient. Many claims have been made and disputed.

This book is not about claims or disputes but about a great food and ingredient worthy of inclusion in our daily food preparation.

Yogurt has much to offer nutritionally but nutrition isn't worth much unless it tastes great. As an ingredient in our cooking, yogurt offers much in the way of flavour and taste without high fat choices.

Making sure you always have some natural yogurt on hand will open a new way of simple, quick and delicious food choices for you. That's what eating is all about.

ISBN 1-877193-15-1

Published in 1997 by
Concept Publishing
Fax 64-9-489 5335
Auckland, New Zealand

Written by
Robyn Martin

Photography by
Alan Gillard

Layout & Type Imaging by
Hot House Design Group Limited

Recipes tested by:
Virginia McGregor
Linda Laycock
Kitchen Assistants:
Rosemary Hurdley
Marie Flynn

Printed in Hong Kong by
Bookprint International Limited

Weights and Measur

All recipes in this book have been teste using New Zealand standard measurin cups and spoons. All cup and spoon measures are level and brown sugar measures are firmly packed.
Standard No 6 eggs are used.

CONTENTS

Step 1
Step 2
FRESH
EASIYO
Real Yogurt
JAR
EASIYO
Fresh Yogurt Making
Base & Culture
MAKES 1 kg
FRESH YOGURT
EASIYO
Fresh Yogurt Making
Base & Culture
MAKES 1 kg
FRESH YOGURT
CONCENTRATED
EASIYO
Flavour for Yogurt
Real Fruit
RASPBERRY
CONCENTRATED
EASIYO
Flavour for Yogurt
Real Fruit
CONCENTRATED
EASIYO
Real Fruit
Flavour for Yogurt
BERRY
FRUITS
435gm Net

SO GOOD FOR YOU

Yogurt is one of the oldest foods known to man. Called by many different names, it was a staple food for many nationalities and its modern form as a flavoured dessert is just one of the ways to present this wonderful natural food.

All yogurt is good for you but fresh yogurt is real yogurt. When properly made and eaten fresh, yogurt is rich in various types of live lactic cultures. These lactobacilli are normally and naturally present in our bodies and they aid in the digestion and assimilation of such nutrients as protein, calcium, iron, phosphorus and potassium. They also create an essential barrier against unhealthy bacteria caused by stress or illness. A daily intake of fresh yogurt helps keep our body in balance.

SO EASY

It has never been so easy to make real yogurt. In 3 easy steps, EASIYO makes perfect yogurt every time. EASIYO yogurt is an all-natural food with no artificial additives. You can eat EASIYO plain or sweetened, or add your favourite EASIYO real fruit flavour. EASIYO is a great alternative as a replacement for milk, cream, sour cream, cream cheese and mayonnaise, in all the following Quick'n'Easy recipes.

YOU WILL LOVE THE TASTE.

EASIYO™

Fresh Yogurt Making

Available in Variety Stores and Supermarkets

EASIYO PRODUCTS LTD
P.O.Box 100 371, N.S.M.C
Auckland, NEW ZEALAND.
Telephone: 9-415 8185
Facsimile: 9-415 8105

Unit 2/180, Kingsgrove Rd
Kingsgrove, NSW 2208
AUSTRALIA.
Telephone: 2-9150 4164
Facsimile: 2-9150 4234

Quick 'n' Easy
DIPS AND NIBBLES

Few people would deny knowledge of reduced cream and packet soup dips and some would even go as far as confessing to eating such combinations.

These mixtures introduced us to the wonderful world of dips and nibbles to serve as pre-dinner snacks with a glass of something.

As tastes, experiences and food choices evolve, different combinations of traditional foods appear and dips and finger foods are no exception.

Yogurt provides a healthy and delicious food base to many pre-dinner snacks as you will see from the recipes that follow.

Choose either full cream yogurt or reduced fat varieties, depending on where you are at. It won't make a scrap of difference to these recipes or the taste.

Quick'n'Easy

Banana Yogurt and Cumin Dip

1 clove garlic
1 small onion
1 tablespoon peanut oil
2 ripe bananas
3 tablespoons lemon juice
1 teaspoon ground cumin
¼ teaspoon salt
Pepper
½ cup Easiyo Natural Yogurt
Fresh coriander

Crush, peel and chop garlic. Peel and chop onion. Heat oil in a frying pan and saute onion and garlic for 5 minutes or until clear. Peel bananas and place with onion and garlic in a blender or food processor. Add lemon juice, cumin, salt and pepper. Process until smooth. Mix in yogurt until combined. Garnish with coriander. Serve with poppadoms.

Makes 2 cups.

Gorgeous Green Salsa

1 avocado
1 clove garlic
1 teaspoon prepared minced chilli
¼ cup roughly chopped parsley
¼ cup coriander leaves
2 tablespoons lime juice
½ cup Easiyo Natural Yogurt

Peel avocado. Remove stone and place flesh in a blender or food processor. Crush and peel garlic. Add to avocado with chilli, parsley, coriander and lime juice. Blend until smooth. Swirl through yogurt and serve with warm pita bread.

Makes 1 cup.

Banana Yogurt and Cumin Dip, Gorgeous Green Salsa

Finger Spinach Pies

250g packet frozen spinach
1 small onion
1 tablespoon oil
1 egg
Pinch ground nutmeg
½ teaspoon salt
Freshly ground black pepper
¼ cup Easiyo Natural Yogurt
3 sheets filo pastry
¼ cup olive oil

Thaw spinach and drain well. Peel onion and chop finely. Heat oil and saute onion for 3 to 4 minutes. Add to spinach with egg, nutmeg, salt, pepper and yogurt. Mix to combine. Lay one sheet of filo pastry on a board. Brush with oil and fold in half lengthwise. Spread a 1cm wide strip of spinach down one long edge of the pastry, to within 1cm from ends. Fold ends in and roll pastry up from the long side. Coil the spinach rolls up, like a snail. Repeat process with the other two sheets of filo and spinach mixture. Place in an oiled roasting dish. Brush with oil and bake at 190°C for 25 minutes or until golden and cooked. Cut into quarters to serve.

Makes 3 coils.

Finger Spinach Pies, Roasted Capsicum and Sundried Tomato Pate, Roasted Aubergine Dip or Spread

Roasted Capsicum and Sundried Tomato Pate

2 red capsicums

½ cup drained sundried tomatoes in oil

1 teaspoon gelatin

1 tablespoon water

½ cup Easiyo Natural Yogurt

Cut capsicums in half. Remove seeds and place cut side down on a baking tray. Grill until skins are golden and blistered. Cool, then remove skins. Place capsicum flesh and tomatoes in a blender or food processor and blend until smooth. Soak the gelatin in the water for 2 to 3 minutes. Dissolve over hot water. Add to capsicum mixture with yogurt and mix until combined. Place in a serving bowl, mould or small loaf tin and serve with vegetables or bread.

Makes 1 ¼ cups.

Roasted Aubergine Dip or Spread

1 medium aubergine

2 tablespoons olive oil

1 small onion

1 clove garlic

½ cup soft white breadcrumbs

¼ cup Easiyo Natural Yogurt

¼ cup finely chopped parsley

Cut aubergine into 1.5cm thick slices. Place on a baking tray. Brush with oil and grill until lightly golden. Turn and brush uncooked side with oil. Grill until golden. Cool, then remove flesh from skin and place in a blender or food processor. Peel onion and chop roughly. Crush and peel garlic. Add onion and garlic to aubergine with breadcrumbs, yogurt and parsley. Blend until combined. Serve with pita crisps.

Makes 1 ¼ cups.

Inspired by Taramosalata

This is something good to make with the few slices of bread that may be left after a visit to the hot bread shop at the weekend.

125g smoked fish roe
1 clove garlic
3 slices stale white bread
Cold water
1 tablespoon finely chopped onion
1 egg yolk
3 tablespoons lemon juice
¼ cup Easiyo Natural Yogurt

Remove skin from roe and place roe in a blender or food processor. Crush and peel garlic. Soak bread in cold water. Drain and squeeze dry. Add garlic, bread, onion, egg yolk and lemon juice to roe. Blend until smooth and combined. Add yogurt and mix until combined. Serve with crisp fresh bread and fresh vegetables.

Makes 1 cup.

Tina Turnovers

2½ sheets pre-rolled flaky pastry
185g can tuna in brine
2 tablespoons chopped chives or spring onion greens
1 teaspoon minced prepared chilli
¼ cup Easiyo Natural Yogurt
1 egg yolk
1 tablespoon water
Poppy seeds

Cut 11cm diameter rounds from pastry sheets. Drain tuna. Mix tuna, chives, chilli and yogurt together. Place a tablespoon of mixture on one half of the pastry round, ½ cm from the edge. Wet pastry edges, fold pastry circles in half over filling and press edges together. Lightly beat egg yolk and water together. Brush over turnovers. Cut a small slash in the top of the turnovers and sprinkle with poppy seeds. Bake at 210°C for 10 minutes or until golden and cooked. Serve warm.

Makes 10.

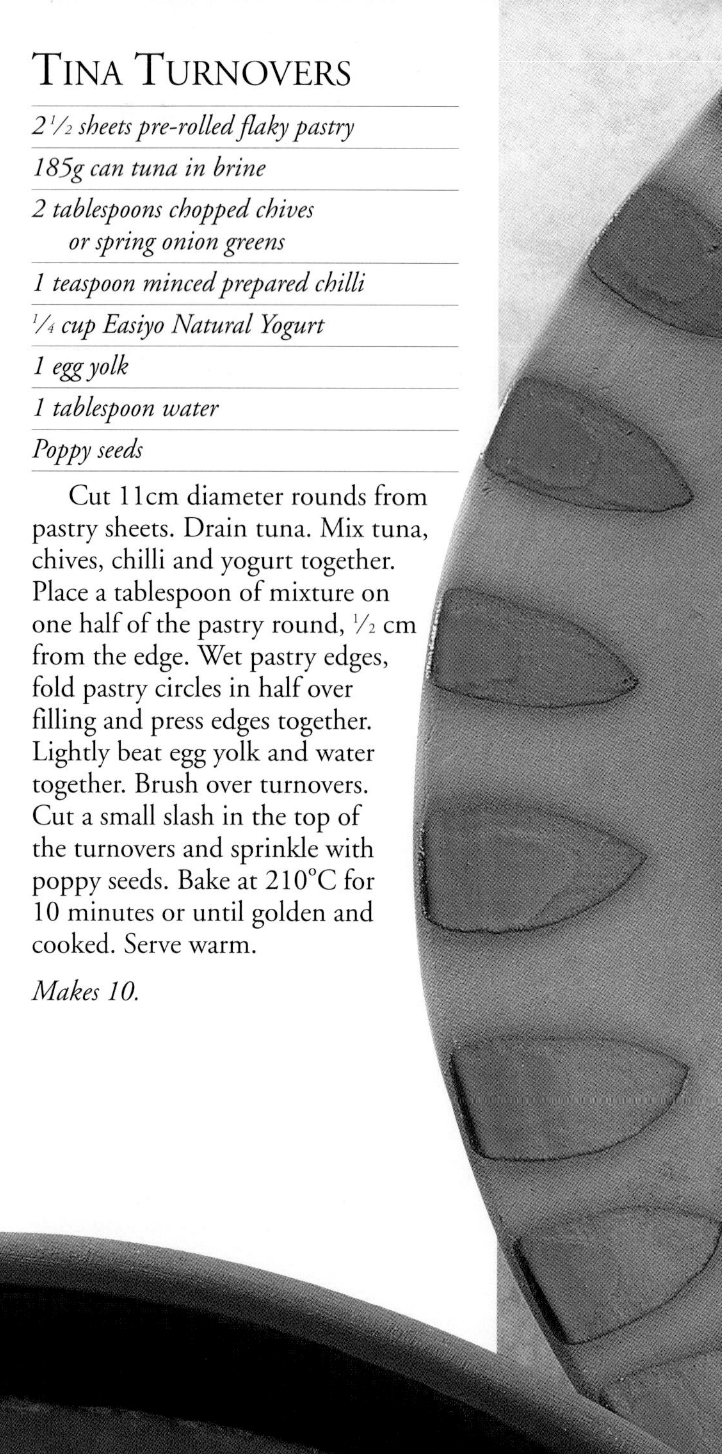

Spicy Topped Pita Bread

2 pita bread rounds
2 cloves garlic
1/4 cup chopped fresh coriander
1 tablespoon lemon juice
1 tablespoon prepared minced chilli
1/2 teaspoon hot curry powder
1/2 cup Easiyo Natural Yogurt

Split pita rounds horizontally. Place cut side up on a baking tray. Grill until lightly golden. Crush, peel and chop garlic. Mix garlic, coriander, lemon juice, chilli, curry powder and yogurt together until combined. Spread over uncut side of pita bread. Grill until golden and dry. Cut into quarters. Serve warm or cold as a snack or dipper.

Makes 16 pieces.

Crisp Pistachio Bread

3 egg whites
2 teaspoons sugar
1 teaspoon ground cumin
1/4 cup chopped pistachios
2 tablespoons Easiyo Natural Yogurt
1/4 cup flour
Freshly ground black pepper

Beat egg whites and sugar together until stiff peaks form. Fold in cumin, pistachios, yogurt, flour and pepper. Spoon into a baking paper-lined 15 x 9cm loaf tin. Bake at 160°C for 45 minutes to 1 hour. To serve, cut loaf into 0.5cm slices. Bake at 160°C for 30 minutes. Serve with dips or spreads.

Inspired by Taramosalata,
Tina Turnovers,
Crisp Pistachio Bread,
Spicy Topped Pita Bread

Potato and Zucchini Fritters with Yogurt Dipping Sauce

2 zucchini
1 medium potato
1 small onion
1 teaspoon dried thyme
2 eggs
1/4 cup flour
1/4 cup oil
YOGURT DIPPING SAUCE
1/2 cup Easiyo Natural Yogurt
1/2 teaspoon dried thyme
1/2 teaspoon grated lemon rind

Trim zucchini and grate. Peel potato and onion and grate. Mix grated vegetables, thyme, eggs and flour together until combined. Heat oil in a large frying pan and cook tablespoonsful of mixture in the oil until golden and cooked on both sides. Drain on absorbent paper. Serve warm with yogurt dipping sauce.

YOGURT DIPPING SAUCE

Mix yogurt, thyme and lemon rind together.

Makes 22 fritters.

Labneh Mak Bus – Very Chic Yogurt Cheese Balls

2 cups Easiyo Natural Yogurt
1 teaspoon salt
4 cloves garlic
2 sprigs rosemary
1/2 cup olives
Olive oil

Mix yogurt and salt together. Line a sieve with two layers of muslin. Place yogurt in this. Place sieve over a bowl and refrigerate for 24 hours to drain. Take tablespoonsful of the drained yogurt and form into balls. Chill until firm. Pack into a sterilised jar. Crush and peel garlic. Add garlic, rosemary and olives to jar and pour over enough olive oil to cover the cheeses. Cover and store in the refrigerator. To serve, remove cheeses from oil, place on a platter and serve with crusty bread.

Makes 12 balls.

MEZZE PLATE OF INTERESTING BITS

TZATZIKI

1 telegraph cucumber

1 teaspoon salt

2 cloves garlic

1 1/2 cups Easiyo Natural Yogurt

1/4 cup chopped fresh mint

Olive oil

Freshly ground black pepper

AUBERGINE CRISPS

1 medium aubergine

Oil for shallow frying

TO SERVE

Black kalamata olives

Pita bread

Shaved pastrami

Fresh herbs

TZATZIKI

Peel cucumber and chop finely. Mix with salt. Set aside for 30 minutes then drain, pressing gently to remove as much liquid as possible. Crush, peel and chop garlic. Mix garlic, yogurt, mint and cucumber together. Place on a serving platter and drizzle with oil. Grind over black pepper.

AUBERGINE CRISPS

Wash aubergine and slice finely. Heat oil in a frying pan and fry aubergine slices a few at a time, until crisp. Drain on absorbent paper.

TO SERVE

Arrange aubergine crisps around tzatziki with olives, warm pita bread and pastrami. Garnish with fresh herbs.

Serves 4.

Potato and Zucchini Fritters with Yogurt Dipping Sauce,
Labneh Mak Bus – Very Chic Yogurt Cheese Balls,
Mezze Plate of Interesting Bits

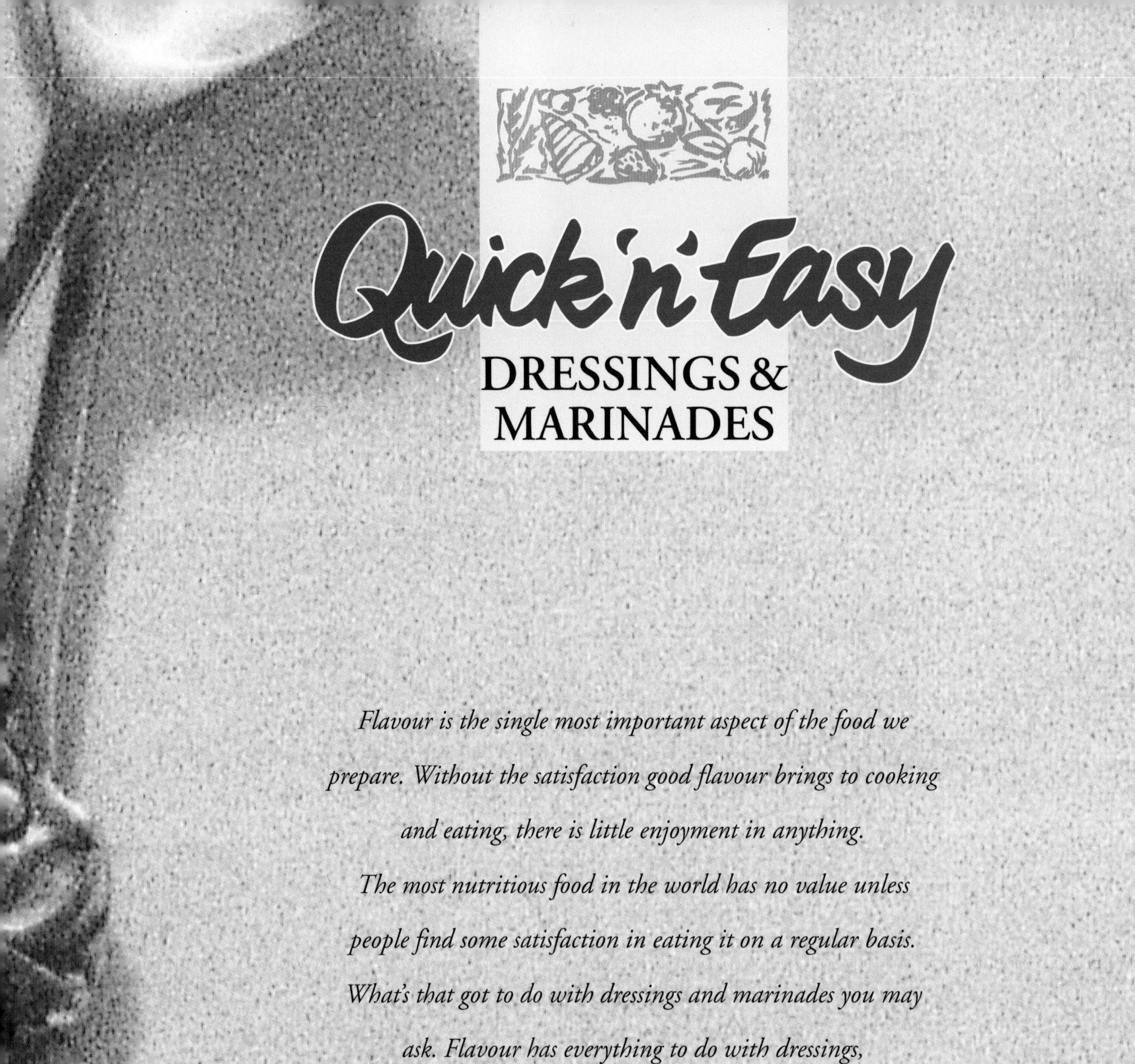

Quick 'n' Easy
DRESSINGS & MARINADES

Flavour is the single most important aspect of the food we prepare. Without the satisfaction good flavour brings to cooking and eating, there is little enjoyment in anything. The most nutritious food in the world has no value unless people find some satisfaction in eating it on a regular basis. What's that got to do with dressings and marinades you may ask. Flavour has everything to do with dressings, sauces and marinades. It's one of these simple combinations that can turn an ordinary lettuce leaf into a taste sensation or a very ordinary piece of meat into a memorable meal.

Cucumber Raita

Serve as an accompaniment to curries, with spicy meat dishes and as a filling for pita bread.

1 small cucumber

1 teaspoon salt

1 tablespoon chopped mint leaves

½ cup Easiyo Natural Yogurt

Peel cucumber then thinly slice flesh. Sprinkle with salt and leave for about 1 hour. Drain well. Rinse under cold running water. Drain well. Mix mint and yogurt into cucumber.

Makes about 1 ½ cups.

Creamy Avocado Dressing

Serve this delicious dressing with nachos, tacos and other Mexican dishes or crisp green or tomato and corn salads.

1 ripe avocado

½ cup Easiyo Natural Yogurt

1 tablespoon tarragon vinegar

1 teaspoon prepared French mustard

Pinch cayenne pepper

½ teaspoon salt

Freshly ground black pepper

Peel avocado. Remove stone. Place avocado flesh in the bowl of a food processor with yogurt, vinegar, mustard and cayenne pepper. Process until smooth. Season with salt and pepper. Serve within an hour.

Makes about 1 cup.

Yogurt Dressing

If you are counting calories or watching your fat intake, try this as a low-fat, low-energy alternative to mayonnaise.

1 cup Easiyo Natural Yogurt

2 tablespoons white wine vinegar

1 tablespoon lemon juice

¼ teaspoon salt

Freshly ground black pepper

Mix yogurt, vinegar, lemon juice, salt and pepper together until combined.

Makes 1 ¼ cups.

Cucumber Raita, Creamy Avocado Dressing, Yogurt Dressing

Magic Mushroom Sauce

This is not a recipe for real magic mushrooms but it tastes so good, you'll have a flavour high. Use a mixture of different mushrooms for this or choose brown "ugly" mushrooms for great flavour. Serve with cooked meats, pasta or polenta dishes.

1 clove garlic
1 small onion
100g mixed mushrooms
1 tablespoon oil
1 teaspoon chopped fresh thyme leaves
½ cup Easiyo Natural Yogurt
2 tablespoons chopped chives
1 tablespoon chopped parsley
½ teaspoon salt
Pepper

Crush, peel and finely chop garlic. Peel and finely chop onion. Wipe mushrooms, then trim and slice. Heat oil in a saucepan and saute onion and garlic for 5 minutes or until onion is clear. Add mushrooms and thyme and cook for about 5 minutes, making sure any liquid evaporates. Add yogurt, chives and parsley and bring to the boil. Season with salt and pepper and serve hot.

Makes about ¾ cup.

Greek Olive Dressing or Baste

Serve with vegetable salads, roasted aubergine and zucchini or use as a baste for chicken or pork.

1 clove garlic
½ roasted capsicum
½ cup chopped green pitted olives
1 tablespoon lemon juice
Pinch cayenne pepper
1 cup Easiyo Natural Yogurt

Crush, peel and finely chop garlic. Cut roasted capsicum into small pieces. Mix garlic, capsicum, olives, lemon juice, cayenne pepper and yogurt together until combined.

Makes about 1¾ cups.

Clockwise from top: Magic Mushroom Sauce, Louisiana Yogurt Dressing, Mustard Dressing, Curried Egg Dressing, Greek Olive Dressing or Baste

Mustard Dressing

This is superb with smoked salmon and potato salads, or used as a dressing for vegetable and pasta salads.

1 cup Easiyo Natural Yogurt
1 tablespoon prepared whole grain mustard
1 tablespoon chopped fresh dill
1/4 teaspoon salt
Freshly ground black pepper

Mix yogurt, mustard, dill, salt and pepper together until combined.

Makes about 1 cup.

Louisiana Yogurt Dressing

Serve with fish or as a vegetable salad dressing.

2 cloves garlic
2 shallots
1 teaspoon tabasco sauce
1 tablespoon white vinegar
1/2 cup Easiyo Natural Yogurt

Crush, peel and finely chop garlic. Peel and finely slice shallots. Mix garlic, shallots, tabasco sauce, vinegar and yogurt together.

Makes about 3/4 cup.

Curried Egg Dressing

This is delicious with fish, pasta and potato salads, with steamed vegetables or a chicken salad.

1 hard-boiled egg
1 tablespoon chopped chives
1 teaspoon curry powder
1 cup Easiyo Natural Yogurt

Shell egg and mouli or chop very, very finely. Mix egg, chives, curry powder and yogurt together. Chill until required.

Makes about 1 1/4 cups.

Quick'n'Easy

Zesty Dressing

Serve with fish and fish cocktail mixtures, steamed green vegetables, baked potatoes and salads.

½ cup mayonnaise
1 cup Easiyo Natural Yogurt
1 teaspoon grated lemon rind
¼ cup finely chopped red onion
½ teaspoon prepared minced chilli
2 tablespoons finely chopped coriander or parsley

Mix the mayonnaise, yogurt, lemon rind, onion, chilli and coriander together until combined. Chill until ready to serve.

Makes about 1½ cups.

Lime and Coriander Yogurt Dressing or Baste

Leave the chilli out of this recipe if you prefer a milder flavour. Serve with salads, chicken or fish or use as a marinade or baste for fish, meat or poultry.

1 cup Easiyo Natural Yogurt
1 teaspoon grated lime rind
2 tablespoons lime juice
3 tablespoons finely chopped fresh coriander
½ teaspoon prepared minced chilli

Mix yogurt, lime rind, juice, coriander and chilli together until combined.

Makes about 1¼ cups.

Zesty Dressing, Lime and Coriander Yogurt Dressing or Baste, Horseradish Dressing, Simple Pesto and Sundried Tomato Dressing

Horseradish Dressing

Serve this with fish, chicken, egg dishes, salads, or use as a marinade or baste for meat, pork or poultry.

1 clove garlic

1 tablespoon prepared hot English mustard

2 tablespoons horseradish cream

1 tablespoon tomato paste

1 cup Easiyo Natural Yogurt

Crush, peel and finely chop garlic. Mix garlic, mustard, horseradish cream, tomato paste and yogurt together until combined. Chill until required.

Makes about 1 1/4 cups.

Simple Pesto and Sundried Tomato Dressing

Use homemade or bought pesto for this recipe and try varying it with other flavoured pestos like coriander or roasted capsicum. Serve with pasta salads or pizza.

1/2 cup Easiyo Natural Yogurt

2 tablespoons basil pesto

1/4 cup finely chopped, drained sundried tomatoes in oil

Mix yogurt, pesto and sundried tomatoes together until combined.

Makes about 3/4 cup.

Yogurt and Mango Sauce or Dressing

Serve this hot with fish, chicken or vegetables or cold as a salad dressing.

1 small onion

1 clove garlic

1 tablespoon oil

1 tablespoon finely chopped root ginger

425g can mangoes

½ cup Easiyo Natural Yogurt

Peel onion and finely chop. Crush, peel and chop garlic. Heat oil in a small saucepan and saute onion, garlic and ginger for 5 minutes until onion is clear. Drain mangoes and puree. Add to saucepan with yogurt. Bring to the boil and serve hot. Alternatively, serve as a dressing, mixing mango puree and yogurt with onion mixture, and serve cold.

Makes about 1 ¼ cups.

Middle Eastern Tahini Yogurt Dressing

Tahini is a sesame seed paste. It is readily available in the supermarket as it's an essential ingredient for making hummus. Serve in pita bread pockets with cold cuts and salad, as a salad dressing or with fresh vegetables as a dip.

1 clove garlic

¼ cup tahini

¼ cup lemon juice

½ cup Easiyo Natural Yogurt

½ teaspoon ground cumin

2 tablespoons chopped parsley

Crush, peel and very finely chop garlic. Mix garlic, tahini, lemon juice, yogurt, cumin and parsley together until combined. If you prefer, do all the chopping and mixing for this dressing in the food processor.

Makes about 1 cup.

Yogurt and Mango Sauce or Dressing, Middle Eastern Tahini Yogurt Dressing

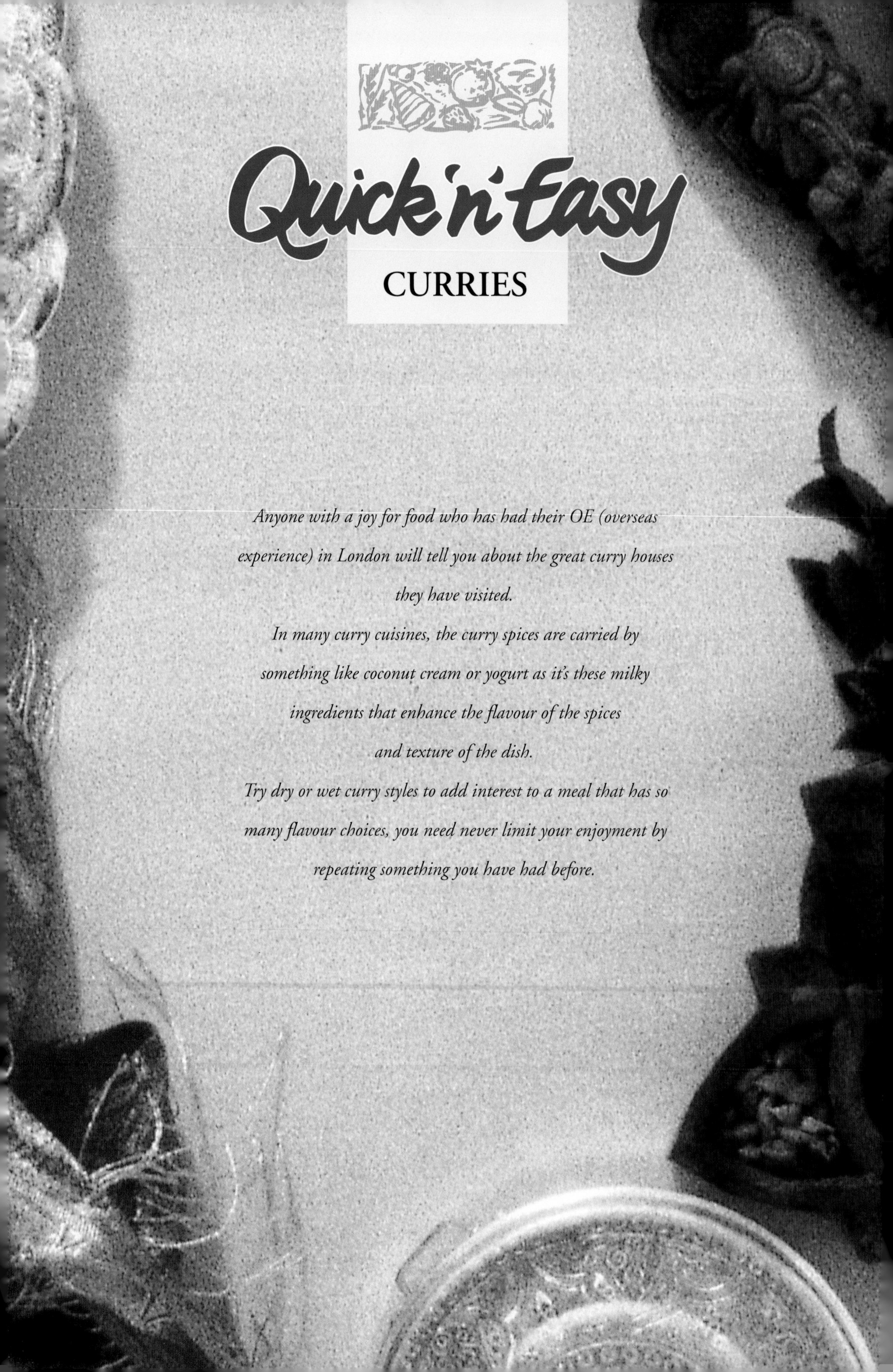

Quick'n'Easy

CURRIES

Anyone with a joy for food who has had their OE (overseas experience) in London will tell you about the great curry houses they have visited.

In many curry cuisines, the curry spices are carried by something like coconut cream or yogurt as it's these milky ingredients that enhance the flavour of the spices and texture of the dish.

Try dry or wet curry styles to add interest to a meal that has so many flavour choices, you need never limit your enjoyment by repeating something you have had before.

VEGETABLE CURRY

500g mixed fresh seasonal vegetables such as pumpkin, parsnip, broccoli, beans, etc
2 onions
1 tablespoon oil
1 tablespoon curry powder
400ml can coconut cream
1 tablespoon sweet chilli sauce
½ cup Easiyo Natural Yogurt
2 tablespoons chopped fresh coriander
1 tablespoon chopped fresh basil

Prepare the vegetables, peeling, trimming and chopping as necessary. Cut into even-sized pieces. Peel onions and chop finely. Heat oil in a saucepan and saute onion for 5 minutes. Add curry powder and saute for 1 minute. Mix in coconut cream. Bring to the boil. Add vegetables. Cover and simmer until vegetables are tender. Mix in chilli sauce and yogurt. Reheat but do not boil. Serve garnished with coriander and basil if wished.

Serves 4 to 6.

BANANA YOGURT SAMBAL

2 bananas
1 tablespoon lemon juice
1 cup Easiyo Natural Yogurt
¼ teaspoon prepared minced chilli
1 tablespoon finely chopped fresh coriander

Peel bananas and cut into 0.5cm cubes. Mix bananas, lemon juice, yogurt, chilli and coriander together. Serve as a curry accompaniment.

Makes 2 cups.

Vegetable Curry, Banana Yogurt Sambal

Tandoori Chicken

Tandoori chicken is traditionally cooked in a special oven called a "tandoor". There are many variations of this recipe so adapt the ingredients to what's in your spice cupboard.

6 single boneless chicken breasts
2 tablespoons lemon juice
1 teaspoon salt
3 cloves garlic
1 cup Easiyo Natural Yogurt
¼ teaspoon ground chilli
1 teaspoon ground ginger
2 teaspoons ground coriander
2 teaspoons ground cumin
½ teaspoon ground cardamom
Freshly ground black pepper
1 teaspoon turmeric

Remove skin from chicken and cut slashes in top of each breast. Sprinkle over lemon juice and salt and set aside while preparing tandoori mix. Crush, peel and finely chop garlic. Mix garlic, yogurt, chilli, ginger, coriander, cumin, cardamom, pepper and turmeric together. Spread mixture all over chicken. Marinate in the refrigerator overnight if possible for the flavours to develop or compromise if needs be and leave at room temperature for about 1 hour. Barbecue or grill chicken until it looks dry on the outside and flesh is cooked, turning during cooking and basting with marinade.

Serves 4 to 6.

Yummy Mango Curried Chicken

4 boneless chicken breasts
½ cup mango chutney
½ cup Easiyo Natural Yogurt
1 tablespoon Madras curry powder
¼ cup roughly chopped blanched peanuts
1 tablespoon chopped parsley or coriander

Remove skin from chicken. Mix chutney, yogurt and curry powder together. Spread over chicken. Place in a roasting dish. Sprinkle peanuts over top of breasts. Bake at 190°C for 25 to 30 minutes or until chicken juices run clear when tested and peanuts are golden. Serve garnished with chopped fresh parsley or coriander.

Serves 4.

Indian Chicken

500g chicken tenderloins
4 cloves garlic
1 onion
1 cup Easiyo Natural Yogurt
2 to 3 tablespoons prepared tandoori paste
1 tablespoon ground coriander
2 teaspoons ground cumin
1 tablespoon grated root ginger
1 tablespoon peanut oil
2 tablespoons tomato paste
1 tablespoon chopped fresh coriander

Cut chicken tenderloins in half lengthwise. Crush, peel and chop garlic. Peel onion and finely chop. Mix yogurt, tandoori paste, coriander, cumin and root ginger together. Toss chicken in this. Marinate for as long as possible. Heat oil in a large frying pan and saute onion and garlic for about 5 minutes until onion is clear. Add chicken mixture and toss quickly, cooking until chicken is cooked. Stir in tomato paste. Serve with raita and poppadams. Garnish with fresh coriander.

Serves 4 to 6.

To Cook Poppadoms in the Microwave

A packet of poppadoms is a great standby to add interest to a simple curry meal. They are traditionally cooked in oil but who can be bothered cleaning up afterwards and, hey, who needs all that extra energy to work off.

POPPADOMS OF ANY FLAVOUR

Place a paper towel on a rack in the microwave. Cook up to 3 poppadoms at a time. Cook on high power for 1 to 2 ½ minutes or until poppadoms crisp all over.

Tandoori Chicken, Yummy Mango Curried Chicken, Indian Chicken

Thai-Style Chicken Curry

This is something I often put together when I need to prepare a meal with speed. Use the concept for your own variation and never be limited by not having a particular ingredient.

2 onions
3 cloves garlic
1 tablespoon peanut oil
1 tablespoon green curry paste
6 boneless chicken thighs
400g can coconut cream
1 medium tomato
½ cup Easiyo Natural Yogurt
2 tablespoons chopped fresh coriander

Peel onions and chop finely. Crush, peel and chop garlic. Heat oil in a medium saucepan and saute onions and garlic for 5 minutes or until onion is clear. Add curry paste and cook for 30 seconds or until paste spices smell fragrant. Skin chicken and cut thighs in half lengthwise. Add to saucepan. Pour in coconut cream. Cover and simmer for 15 to 20 minutes or until chicken is cooked. Cut tomato in half. Remove core and cut flesh into cubes. Add to chicken with yogurt and coriander. Bring to boiling point but do not boil. Serve with steamed rice.

Serves 4 to 6.

Thai-Style Chicken Curry, Leg of Lamb Masala, Curried Fish Stew

Leg of Lamb Masala

Try this for a new angle to a lamb roast.

1 leg lamb
4 cloves garlic
1 teaspoon turmeric
½ teaspoon ground chilli
1 teaspoon garam masala
2 tablespoons chopped fresh mint
2 tablespoons chopped fresh coriander
½ teaspoon salt
1 cup Easiyo Natural Yogurt

Trim fat from lamb, removing skin as you do so. Cut 5 to 6 slashes in lamb. Crush and peel garlic. Place garlic, turmeric, chilli, garam masala, mint, coriander, salt and yogurt in a blender and blend until smooth. Spread over lamb, taking the mixture into the cuts. Refrigerate overnight if possible. If not, roast straightaway at 180°C for 1½ to 2 hours depending on how you like your lamb cooked.

Serves 6.

Curried Fish Stew

4 skinned and boned fillets white fleshed fish
1 onion
2 cloves garlic
1 tablespoon oil
1 tablespoon prepared minced chilli
1 teaspoon ground ginger
1 teaspoon turmeric
1 cup fish stock
1 cup Easiyo Natural Yogurt
Salt

Cut fish into large chunks. Peel onion and chop finely. Crush, peel and finely chop garlic. Heat oil in a medium saucepan and saute onion and garlic for 5 minutes or until clear. Mix chilli, ginger and turmeric together and add to pan. Saute until spices smell fragrant. Add fish stock. Bring to the boil then add fish. Simmer for 10 minutes or until fish is cooked. Stir in yogurt, bring to boiling point but do not boil. Season with salt and serve hot.

Serves 4.

Spicy Yogurt Rice

This is a traditional Southern Indian rice dish served at room temperature as a curry accompaniment. You may have to go to a speciality food store to buy the mustard seeds or try a health food shop.

- *1 cup long grain rice*
- *4 cups water*
- *1 cup Easiyo Natural Yogurt*
- *1 teaspoon salt*
- *2 green chillies*
- *2 tablespoons grated root ginger*
- *1 tablespoon peanut oil*
- *1 tablespoon black mustard seeds*
- *2 tablespoons chopped fresh coriander*

Wash rice. Cook in measured boiling water for 12 minutes or until tender. Drain well. Mix in yogurt and salt while rice is hot. Cut chillies lengthwise. Remove seeds and slice flesh thinly. Mix chillies and ginger through rice mixture. Heat oil in a frying pan and carefully pop mustard seeds over a low heat. Add to rice with coriander. Mix until combined.

Serves 4.

Apple and Coconut Chutney

Good old Granny Smith apples are good for this recipe but use what is abundant at the time.

- *1 apple*
- *2 spring onions*
- *1 clove garlic*
- *1/4 cup coconut*
- *1/2 teaspoon sugar*
- *1 teaspoon grated root ginger*
- *1 tablespoon cider vinegar*
- *1 cup Easiyo Natural Yogurt*
- *1 tablespoon chopped fresh coriander*

Peel apple, core and grate coarsely. Trim spring onions and slice finely. Crush, peel and finely chop garlic. Mix apple, spring onions, garlic, coconut, sugar, ginger, vinegar, yogurt and coriander together. Chill until required. Serve as a curry accompaniment.

Makes 1 1/4 cups.

Spiced Potatoes with Yogurt and Coconut

6 potatoes

1 tablespoon prepared minced chilli

1 teaspoon ground coriander

1 teaspoon ground cumin

½ teaspoon turmeric

½ teaspoon salt

½ teaspoon whole yellow mustard seeds

Pinch cayenne pepper

3 tablespoons peanut oil

2 tablespoons lime juice

½ cup Easiyo Natural Yogurt

¼ cup toasted coconut

Peel potatoes. Cut into 2cm cubes. Cook in boiling salted water until just tender. Drain well. Mix chilli, coriander, cumin, turmeric, salt, mustard seeds and cayenne pepper together. Heat oil in a large frying pan and add spices, cooking for a few minutes until spices smell fragrant. Add potatoes, cooking over a medium heat until potatoes start to brown. Transfer to a serving dish. Mix lime juice and yogurt together. Pour over potatoes. Garnish with toasted coconut.

Serves 4.

Spiced Potatoes with Yogurt and Coconut,
Apple and Coconut Chutney,
Spicy Yogurt Rice

Quick Indian Griddle Cakes

2 tablespoons lukewarm water
¼ teaspoon sugar
1 teaspoon dried yeast
½ cup flour suitable for breadmaking
½ cup self-raising flour
½ cup ground rice
2 tablespoons semolina
1 cup Easiyo Natural Yogurt
¾ cup warm water
1 onion
1 tablespoon chopped root ginger
1 tablespoon prepared minced chilli
1 tablespoon sesame or peanut oil

Mix first measure of water and sugar together. Sprinkle yeast over and leave for 10 minutes until frothy. Sift flour, self-raising flour, rice and semolina into a bowl. Mix yogurt and second measure of water together. Mix yeast mixture and yogurt into flour mixture, beating with a wooden spoon until smooth. Cover and set aside while preparing remaining ingredients. Peel onion and chop finely. Mix onion, ginger and chilli together and mix into batter. Oil a frying pan with sesame or peanut oil. Cook half cupful of batter at a time in a hot pan, turning to cook the other side when golden. Serve warm topped with meat or chicken curries, spicy nut mixtures or vegetables.

Makes 7.

INDIAN FISH CAKES WITH CORIANDER AND LIME SAUCE

425g can tuna in brine
2 teaspoons ground cumin
2 teaspoons ground coriander
1 tablespoon prepared minced chilli
3 eggs
2 tablespoons cornflour
2 tablespoons chopped fresh coriander
1 tablespoon butter
CORIANDER AND LIME SAUCE
1 small red onion
2 tablespoons chopped fresh coriander
1 teaspoon grated lime rind
2 teaspoons prepared minced chilli
1 cup Easiyo Natural Yogurt

Drain tuna. Mix tuna, cumin, coriander, chilli, eggs, cornflour and fresh coriander together until combined. Melt butter in a frying pan and cook quarter cupsful of mixture until golden on one side, then turn and cook second side. Serve hot with Coriander and Lime Sauce.

CORIANDER AND LIME SAUCE

Peel onion and chop finely. Mix onion, coriander, lime rind, chilli and yogurt together until combined.

Serves 4.

Quick Indian Griddle Cakes, Indian Fish Cakes with Coriander and Lime Sauce

Quick 'n' Easy
LIGHT MEALS

Many occasions call for something deliciously smart, yet light and easy to prepare.

Perhaps it's a casual Sunday night tea for family or friends or a luncheon or alfresco meal you have to prepare with minimum fuss but maximum eating enjoyment.

Yogurt provides such a good starting point for so many meals and a light, delicious meal is no exception.

Quick Ham and Asparagus Lasagne

2 x 425g cans asparagus spears

1 cup Easiyo Natural Yogurt

Freshly ground black pepper

400g packet fresh lasagne

200g shaved ham

1 cup Easiyo Natural Yogurt

2 eggs

1 cup grated tasty cheese

Drain asparagus. Mix asparagus spears with first measure of yogurt and season with pepper. Cut lasagne to fit a 27 x 18cm oiled lasagne dish. Place a sheet of lasagne in the bottom of the dish. Spread with a thin layer of asparagus mixture. Arrange a layer of shaved ham over the top of the asparagus. Repeat layers, finishing with a layer of lasagne. Mix yogurt and eggs together until combined. Pour over lasagne. Sprinkle with cheese and bake at 180°C for 25 minutes.

Serves 4 to 6.

Bengal Pizza

Buy a pizza base for this recipe or use pita bread or make your own pizza base using the Quick Pizza Dough featured in my *Quick 'n' Easy Italian* or *Fast Finger Food* books.

1 x 29cm pizza base

2 tablespoons green curry paste

1 tablespoon chilli oil

350g chicken tenderloins

½ cup fruit chutney

8 cucumber slices

½ cup Easiyo Natural Yogurt

¼ cup chopped fresh coriander

Spread pizza base with curry paste to within 1cm from edge. Grill for about 2 minutes or until hot. Heat oil in a frying pan and cook tenderloins for 2 to 3 minutes or until cooked through. Top hot pizza base with chicken. Spoon chutney into the middle of the pizza with the cucumber. Mix yogurt and coriander together. Spoon over centre of pizza and serve immediately.

Serves 2 to 4.

Quick Ham and Asparagus Lasagne, Bengal Pizza

Scrambled Eggs with Yogurt and Chives

Making scrambled eggs with yogurt adds a new dimension to this simple, popular dish.

2 eggs

2 tablespoons Easiyo Natural Yogurt

2 tablespoons finely chopped chives

Salt

Freshly ground black pepper

1/2 teaspoons butter

2 slices wholegrain toast

Lightly beat eggs and yogurt together until combined. Mix in chives, salt and pepper. Melt butter in a small frying pan. Pour in egg mixture and cook over a medium heat until beginning to set. Drag a wooden spoon through mixture to let uncooked mixture run through to cook. The mixture should form large clots. Serve with wholegrain toast.

Serves 1.

Mashed Potatoes with Poached Eggs and Smoked Salmon

If you haven't got fresh dill for this recipe, use parsley.

4 medium potatoes

1/2 cup Easiyo Natural Yogurt

4 eggs

1 tablespoon vinegar

100g packet smoked salmon slices

1/4 cup Easiyo Natural Yogurt

2 tablespoons chopped fresh dill

Freshly ground black pepper

Peel potatoes. Cut into even-sized pieces and cook in boiling salted water until tender. Drain, reserving 1/4 cup cooking water. Mash potatoes with reserved cooking water. Beat in enough of the first measure of yogurt to make potatoes smooth and creamy. Poach eggs in simmering water with vinegar added. Drain well. Arrange mashed potato on four serving plates. Top with a poached egg and serve with smoked salmon slices. Mix second measure of yogurt and dill together. Spoon over egg and salmon. Grind over black pepper.

Serves 4.

Spinach and Salmon Roulade

250g packet frozen spinach
50g butter
¼ cup flour
1 cup Easiyo Natural Yogurt
4 eggs
½ teaspoon salt
¼ teaspoon ground nutmeg
Easiyo Natural Yogurt to serve
FILLING
210g can pink salmon
½ cup Easiyo Natural Yogurt

Thaw spinach. Drain well, squeezing out as much water as possible. Chop spinach finely. Melt butter in a saucepan. Add flour and cook until frothy. Remove from heat and stir in yogurt. Return to heat and bring to the boil. Cool. Separate eggs and mix yolks, spinach, salt and nutmeg into yogurt sauce. Beat egg whites until stiff. Fold spinach mix into this. Pour into a baking paper-lined 32 x 22cm sponge roll tin. Bake at 200°C for 15 minutes. Turn onto a clean tea-towel. Remove baking paper and roll up from the long side using the tea-towel to help. Cool. Unroll and fill with yogurt mixture. Re-roll. Serve sliced with extra yogurt if wished.

FILLING

Drain salmon. Remove skin and bones. Mix with yogurt.

Serves 4 to 6.

Scrambled Eggs with Yogurt and Chives, Mashed Potatoes with Poached Eggs and Smoked Salmon, Spinach and Salmon Roulade

Quick'n'Easy

Savoury Mexican Bake

The chilli beans weren't hot enough for our palate, so we added extra chilli.

1 onion
2 cloves garlic
1 tablespoon oil
400g can Mexican tomatoes
420g can chilli beans
1/4 to 1/2 teaspoon chilli powder
1/2 cup grated tasty cheese
TOPPING
3/4 cup fine cornmeal
2 teaspoons baking powder
1/2 teaspoon salt
2 eggs
1/2 cup Easiyo Natural Yogurt

Peel onion and chop finely. Crush, peel and chop garlic. Heat oil in a frying pan and saute onion and garlic for 5 minutes or until clear. Add tomatoes, chilli beans and chilli powder. Pour into the bottom of a 5 cup capacity ovenproof dish. Pour over topping, sprinkle with cheese and bake at 200°C for 20 minutes or until topping is golden and set. Serve hot with a green salad.

TOPPING

Mix cornmeal, baking power and salt together. Lightly beat eggs and mix in yogurt. Mix into dry ingredients. Pour over bean mixture.

Serves 4.

Savoury Mexican Bake, Yummy Chilli Cornbread, Fish and Rice Soup

Yummy Chilli Cornbread

This is in the light meal chapter for the simple reason I didn't know where else to put it as it was too substantial for a nibble and too delicious to be left out. Form a light meal around it or serve it as a meal accompaniment.

1 cup fine cornmeal

1 ½ cups flour

3 teaspoons baking powder

1 teaspoon salt

2 eggs

1 tablespoon prepared minced chilli

440g can drained whole kernel corn

2 cups Easiyo Natural Yogurt

Mix cornmeal, flour, baking powder and salt together in a bowl. Lightly beat eggs and chilli together. Mix in corn and yogurt. Make a well in the centre of the dry ingredients and mix quickly until ingredients are just mixed. Pour into a baking paper-lined 14 x 24cm loaf tin. Bake at 180°C for 1 hour or until loaf springs back when lightly touched. Serve warm with a salad and cold cuts.

Fish and Rice Soup

1 onion

1 clove garlic

25g butter

6 cups fish stock

1 cup long grain rice

200g mixed fish such as prawns, scallops, mussels and white-fleshed fish fillets

1 cup Easiyo Natural Yogurt

2 tablespoons chopped parsley

Peel onion and chop finely. Crush, peel and chop garlic. Melt butter and saute onion and garlic until onion is clear. Add fish stock and bring to the boil. Add rice. Cover and cook for 7 minutes. Prepare fish as necessary, cutting fillets into cubes. Add to soup and cook for 4 minutes or until rice and fish are cooked. Stir in yogurt. Bring to the boil but do not boil. Mix in parsley and serve.

Serves 4.

Light-on-Fat Chilled Savoury Cheesecake

Oil
½ cup dried breadcrumbs
2 cloves garlic
500g pot cottage cheese
2 cups Easiyo Natural Yogurt
½ cup lemon juice
1 cup roughly chopped mixture of parsley, dill and chives
¼ cup drained sundried tomatoes in oil
1 teaspoon salt
2 tablespoons gelatin
¼ cup cold water
200g packet hot smoked salmon
Fresh herbs

Generously oil the base and sides of a 20cm spring-form pan. Pour in the breadcrumbs and turn pan to coat base and sides. Crush and peel garlic. Place garlic, cottage cheese, yogurt, lemon juice and herbs in a blender or food processor. Process until smooth. Chop sundried tomatoes and mix into yoghurt mixture. Season with salt. Soak gelatin in water for 5 minutes. Stand over hot water and stir until dissolved. Mix into yogurt mixture. Pour half the yogurt mixture into the spring-form pan. Refrigerate until the consistency of raw egg white. Flake smoked salmon and arrange over partially set yoghurt mixture. Top with remaining yogurt mixture and refrigerate until set. Remove from tin to serve. Garnish with fresh herbs and serve with crusty bread and a salad.

Serves 6.

Onion Tart

Make individual ones of these if you have small tart tins.

400g packet savoury short pastry
FILLING
4 large onions
2 cloves garlic
2 tablespoons oil
3 eggs
1 cup Easiyo Natural Yogurt
¼ cup chopped chives

Roll pastry out on a lightly floured board to 0.5cm thickness and use to line a 35cm flan dish or tin. Line with baking paper, fill with baking blind beans and bake at 190°C for 10 minutes. Remove baking blind material and return pastry case to oven for 3 minutes to dry. Cool while preparing filling. Arrange onions over pastry base. Pour over egg mixture. Bake at 180°C for 25 minutes or until filling is set. Serve warm with a green salad.

FILLING

Peel onions and slice thinly. Crush, peel and chop garlic. Heat oil in a frying pan and saute onions and garlic for 5 to 10 minutes or until lightly golden. Beat eggs with a fork and mix in yogurt and chives.

Serves 4 to 6.

Onion Tart, Light-on-Fat Chilled Savoury Cheesecake

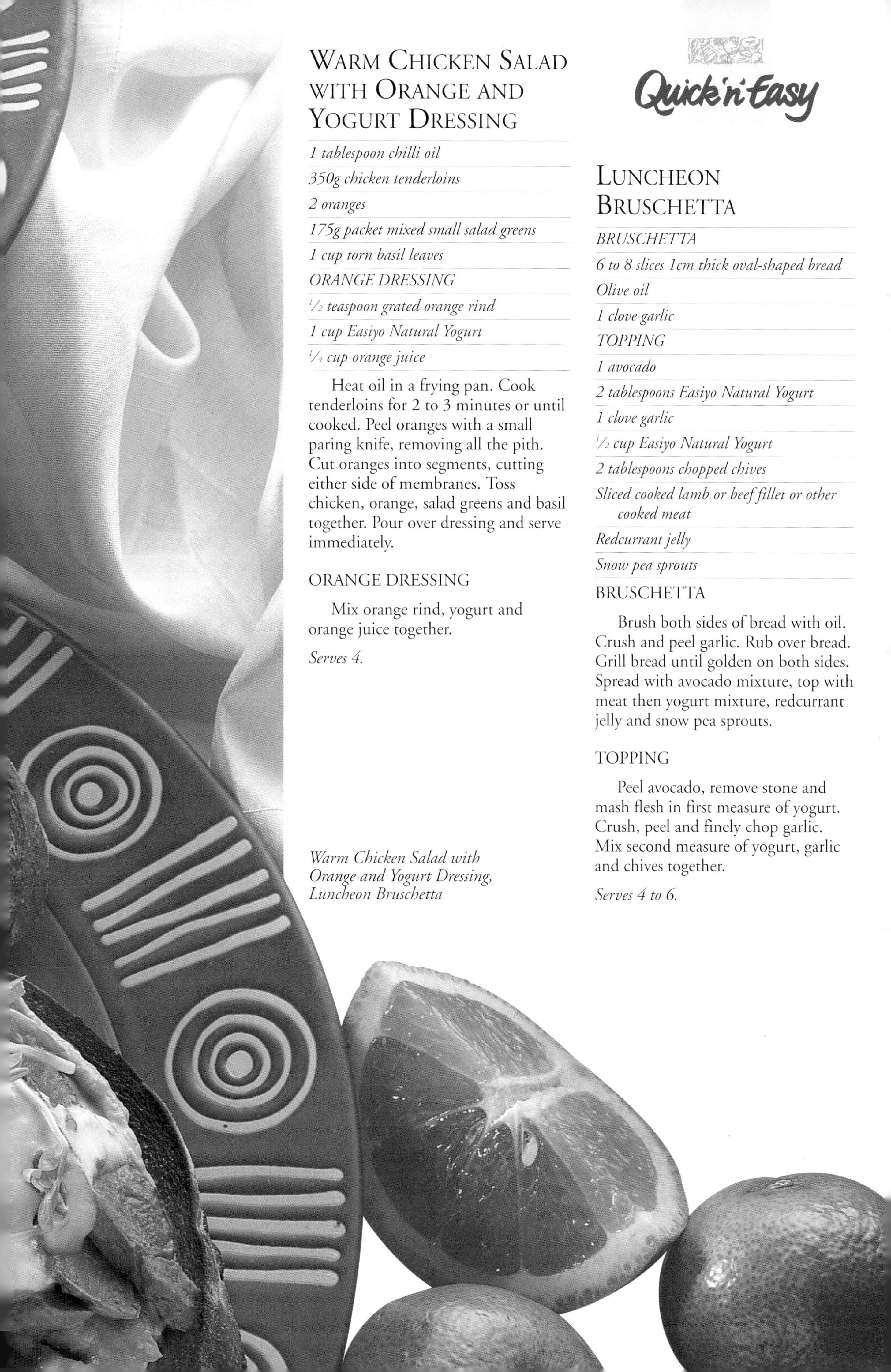

Warm Chicken Salad with Orange and Yogurt Dressing

1 tablespoon chilli oil

350g chicken tenderloins

2 oranges

175g packet mixed small salad greens

1 cup torn basil leaves

ORANGE DRESSING

½ teaspoon grated orange rind

1 cup Easiyo Natural Yogurt

¼ cup orange juice

Heat oil in a frying pan. Cook tenderloins for 2 to 3 minutes or until cooked. Peel oranges with a small paring knife, removing all the pith. Cut oranges into segments, cutting either side of membranes. Toss chicken, orange, salad greens and basil together. Pour over dressing and serve immediately.

ORANGE DRESSING

Mix orange rind, yogurt and orange juice together.

Serves 4.

Warm Chicken Salad with Orange and Yogurt Dressing, Luncheon Bruschetta

Luncheon Bruschetta

BRUSCHETTA

6 to 8 slices 1cm thick oval-shaped bread

Olive oil

1 clove garlic

TOPPING

1 avocado

2 tablespoons Easiyo Natural Yogurt

1 clove garlic

½ cup Easiyo Natural Yogurt

2 tablespoons chopped chives

Sliced cooked lamb or beef fillet or other cooked meat

Redcurrant jelly

Snow pea sprouts

BRUSCHETTA

Brush both sides of bread with oil. Crush and peel garlic. Rub over bread. Grill bread until golden on both sides. Spread with avocado mixture, top with meat then yogurt mixture, redcurrant jelly and snow pea sprouts.

TOPPING

Peel avocado, remove stone and mash flesh in first measure of yogurt. Crush, peel and finely chop garlic. Mix second measure of yogurt, garlic and chives together.

Serves 4 to 6.

Quick'n'Easy MAIN COURSES

Gone are the days when rich, creamy sauces and a knob of butter added here and there to everyday meals was the norm. Modern meals require plenty of speed in preparation, great taste and good nutrition. Enlightened cooks don't need the addition of ingredients high in fat to make the difference between a memorable and everyday meal. Anything from a pasta sauce to a casserole is enhanced by the use of yogurt as an ingredient and with varieties made from full cream or reduced-fat milk available, it's up to us which path we choose.

Salmon and Yogurt Pasta Sauce

1 onion
2 cloves garlic
1 tablespoon oil
3 fresh salmon steaks
1 cup Easiyo Natural Yogurt
2 tablespoons roasted capsicum pesto
2 tablespoons chopped parsley
300g penne pasta
Fresh herbs

Peel onion and chop finely. Crush, peel and chop garlic. Heat oil in a frying pan and saute onion and garlic for 5 minutes or until onion is clear. Set aside. Add salmon steaks to pan and cook for 2 minutes each side or until just cooked. Cut salmon into chunks, removing skin and bones. Mix yogurt, pesto, onion, garlic and parsley together. Cook penne to packet directions. Drain well. Toss through yogurt mixture, top with salmon and garnish with fresh herbs. Serve immediately.

Serves 3 to 4.

Smoked Fish Filo Pie

500g smoked fish
2 spring onions
1 tablespoon chopped parsley
1 teaspoon grated lemon rind
1 ½ cups Easiyo Natural Yogurt
6 sheets filo pastry
2 teaspoons melted butter
Poppy seeds

Remove fish flesh from bones and skin and flake. Trim spring onions and slice finely. Mix fish, spring onions, parsley, lemon rind and yogurt together. Place in an ovenproof dish. Crumple up filo pastry and place over top of fish mixture. Brush with melted butter. Sprinkle with poppy seeds. Bake at 200°C for 15 minutes or until pastry is golden.

Serves 4.

Salmon and Yogurt Pasta Sauce, Smoked Fish Filo Pie

Roasted Pumpkin Gnocchi with Basil Yogurt Sauce

This is the sort of dish you make the night after you have roasted extra pumpkin when cooking an earlier meal.

300g piece pumpkin
2 egg yolks
1 tablespoon Easiyo Natural Yogurt
Salt
Freshly ground black pepper
About ¼ cup flour
Sprig fresh basil
BASIL YOGURT SAUCE
½ cup finely chopped fresh basil
1 cup Easiyo Natural Yogurt
2 tablespoons lemon juice

Peel and deseed pumpkin. Cut into even-sized pieces and roast at 180°C for 30 to 40 minutes or until cooked. Puree pumpkin in a food processor or blender. Add egg yolks, yogurt, salt and pepper and enough flour to make a stiff dough that leaves the side of the bowl. Break off tablespoonfuls of mixture. Shape into ovals and cook in boiling water until gnocchi float to the surface. Remove from water with a slotted spoon, straining well. Place in a serving bowl. Pour over basil yogurt sauce and grill until lightly browned. Serve garnished with a sprig of fresh basil.

BASIL YOGURT SAUCE

Mix the basil, yogurt and lemon juice together in a small saucepan. Bring to the boil but do not boil.

Serves 4.

Roasted Pumpkin Gnocchi with Basil Yogurt Sauce, Lemon Chicken, Spinach and Yogurt Fish Fillets

Lemon Chicken

4 single chicken breasts
½ cup Easiyo Natural Yogurt
2 tablespoons lemon juice
2 teaspoons grated lemon rind
1 tablespoon cornflour
1 teaspoon ground turmeric
1 tablespoon chopped parsley
½ teaspoon salt
Freshly ground black pepper

Remove skin from chicken. Place in an ovenproof dish. Mix yogurt, lemon juice, rind, cornflour, turmeric and parsley together. Season with salt and pepper. Pour over chicken, turning breasts to coat. Bake at 180°C for 25 minutes or until chicken is cooked. Serve with steamed rice or pasta.

Serves 4.

Spinach and Yogurt Fish Fillets

450g packet frozen spinach
1 onion
2 cloves garlic
25g butter
2 tablespoons flour
1 cup dry white wine
1 cup Easiyo Natural Yogurt
4 fish fillets
Lemon slices

Thaw spinach. Squeeze out as much water as possible. Peel onion and chop finely. Crush, peel and finely chop garlic. Melt butter in a saucepan. Saute onion and garlic for 5 minutes or until onion is clear. Stir in flour and cook until frothy. Stir in wine and cook until sauce boils and thickens. Finely chop spinach and add to sauce with yogurt. Bring to the boil and simmer for 3 minutes. Fry or poach fish fillets. Place on a serving plate, pour over spinach sauce and serve garnished with lemon slices.

Serves 4.

Veal Paprika

4 beef schnitzels
2 tablespoons oil
1 onion
2 cloves garlic
1 1/2 tablespoons paprika
1 teaspoon salt
2 tablespoons flour
1 1/2 cups beef stock
1 tablespoon tomato paste
3/4 cup Easiyo Natural Yogurt
Chopped parsley

Trim schnitzel into even-sized pieces. Heat oil in a frying pan and brown meat on both sides. Remove from pan. Peel onion and chop finely. Crush, peel and chop garlic. Saute onion and garlic in frying pan for 5 minutes or until clear. Add paprika, salt and flour. Gradually stir in the stock, stirring until the mixture boils and thickens. Stir in the tomato paste. Add the meat to the sauce. Cover and simmer for 25 minutes. Stir in the yogurt. Bring to the boil but do not boil. Place in a serving dish and garnish with chopped parsley.

Serves 4.

Veal Paprika,
Coconut-Covered Pork Schnitzel

Coconut-Covered Pork Schnitzel

This is a great way of cooking schnitzel without using heaps of oil. The schnitzel size will determine how many you need.

4 to 6 pieces pork schnitzel
2 tablespoons mango chutney
½ cup Easiyo Natural Yogurt
1 tablespoon cornflour
About 1½ cups coconut
4 small unpeeled bananas

Trim any fat from pork schnitzel. Mix chutney, yogurt and cornflour together in a shallow bowl. Dip schnitzel in this to coat both sides. Coat with coconut. Place in an oiled roasting dish. Wash and dry unpeeled bananas. Place in dish with schnitzel. Bake at 190°C for 10 minutes, turning halfway through cooking.

Serves 4.

Across the Vines Albanian Lamb Casserole

Recipe ideas are often exchanged when people chat while performing menial tasks. During a wonderful day of grape-picking in a friend's vineyard, this recipe idea was shared.

1kg lamb shoulder steaks
2 cups water
2 carrots
1 large parsnip
4 stalks celery
2 teaspoons black peppercorns
5 bay leaves
TOPPING
3 eggs
2 tablespoons flour
1 cup Easiyo Natural Yogurt
$\frac{1}{2}$ teaspoon salt
$1\frac{1}{2}$ cups reserved cooking stock

Place meat in a medium saucepan. Add water and bring to the boil, skimming off the scum that forms. Peel the carrots and parsnip and trim the celery. When the water is clear of scum, add the vegetables, peppercorns and one bay leaf to the meat. Cover and simmer gently for $1\frac{1}{2}$ hours or until the meat is cooked. Cut meat into cubes, place in 4 ovenproof bowls. Strain stock, discarding vegetables and leave until lukewarm. Pour topping over meat. Place a bay leaf on top of each dish. Bake at 180°C for 20 minutes or until the topping is lightly set.

TOPPING

Lightly beat eggs. Beat in flour, yogurt, salt and reserved stock.

Serves 4 to 6.

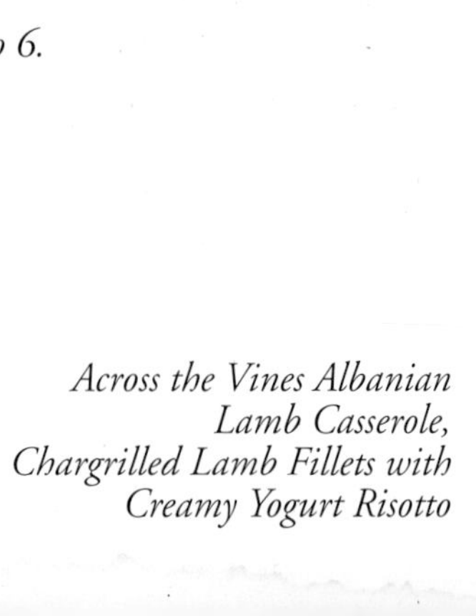

Across the Vines Albanian Lamb Casserole, Chargrilled Lamb Fillets with Creamy Yogurt Risotto

Chargrilled Lamb Fillets with Creamy Yogurt Risotto

RISOTTO

1 onion

2 cloves garlic

25g butter

1 cup arborio rice

4 cups chicken stock

Salt

½ cup Easiyo Natural Yogurt

1 roasted red capsicum

Fresh herbs

LAMB FILLETS

6 lamb fillets

Oil

YOGURT SAUCE

½ cup Easiyo Natural Yogurt

1 tablespoon red wine or balsamic vinegar

1 tablespoon chopped parsley

RISOTTO

Peel onion and chop finely. Crush, peel and finely chop garlic. Melt butter in a large frying pan and saute onion and garlic for 5 minutes or until clear. Add rice and saute until clear and coated with butter. Add one cup of stock and stir until liquid has evaporated. Add stock, half a cup at a time, and continue to cook, stirring until rice is cooked and stock has evaporated. Season with salt and mix in yogurt. Cut capsicum into thin strips and mix through. To serve, place a round of risotto in the centre of 4 hot serving plates. Arrange lamb in a stack over risotto. Serve with yogurt sauce and garnish with fresh herbs.

LAMB FILLETS

Brush lamb with oil. Cook lamb in a frying pan, under the grill or over the barbecue for 2 to 3 minutes or until just cooked.

YOGURT SAUCE

Mix yogurt, vinegar and parsley together.

Serves 4.

Filo Lamb Parcels

8 lamb steaks

2 tablespoons olive oil

1 onion

1 clove garlic

1 tablespoon tomato paste

1 cup Easiyo Natural Yogurt

1 tablespoon chopped fresh sage or 1½ teaspoons dried sage

8 sheets filo pastry

Melted butter

Fresh sage

Trim fat from meat and cut meat into even-sized pieces. Heat oil in a frying pan and brown meat on both sides. Drain on absorbent paper. Peel onion and finely chop. Crush, peel and chop garlic. Add to pan meat was cooked in and saute for 5 minutes. Mix onion, garlic, tomato paste, yogurt and sage together. Cut filo in half crosswise. Cover with a damp tea-towel. Place a piece of filo on a board. Brush with melted butter, top with a second sheet on the diagonal to the first piece. Place a piece of meat in the centre of the filo pastry. Top with a quarter of the yogurt mixture. Gather filo pastry around meat mixture, bunching up to form a parcel. Place on a greased oven tray. Bake at 190°C for 15 to 20 minutes or until golden.

Serves 4.

Filo Lamb Parcels, Koftas, Moroccan Leg of Lamb

Koftas

1 onion

1 clove garlic

500g lean beef or lamb mince

2 tablespoons chopped fresh mint

1 teaspoon salt

2 teaspoons ground cumin

½ teaspoon ground allspice

¼ cup Easiyo Natural Yogurt

Oil

4 small pita bread

Lettuce

Tomato

½ cup Easiyo Natural Yogurt

2 tablespoons tahini

Peel onion and grate. Squeeze out juice. Crush, peel and chop garlic. Mix onion, garlic, mince, mint, salt, cumin, allspice and first measure of yogurt together until combined. With wet hands, shape into 5cm long cylinders. Thread onto soaked satay sticks or metal skewers. Brush with oil and grill or barbecue until golden and cooked. Warm pita bread in the oven or microwave. Slit to make a pocket. Fill with lettuce, tomato and a kofta. Mix second measure of yogurt with tahini and spoon into pita pocket.

Serves 4.

Moroccan Leg of Lamb

1 onion

2 cloves garlic

½ cup chopped parsley

¼ cup chopped fresh coriander

1 tablespoon prepared minced chilli

1 teaspoon ground cumin

1 teaspoon grated lemon rind

2 tablespoons lemon juice

1 cup Easiyo Natural Yogurt

Boned leg of lamb

Peel onion and chop finely. Crush, peel and finely chop garlic. Mix onion, garlic, parsley, coriander, chilli, cumin, lemon rind, juice and yogurt together. Open out lamb and spread this mixture over the cut surface of the meat. Close and spread on outside of lamb. Refrigerate overnight if possible. Barbecue or roast at 180°C for 45 to 60 minutes or until lamb is cooked to your preference. Slice thinly to serve.

Serves 6.

Quick 'n' Easy SWEET TREATS

It wasn't that long ago that the great unwashed considered a yogurt and muesli-eating breakfast eater to be a definite candidate for a health farm.

Now yogurt, fruit and muesli combinations are staple fare to say nothing of using yogurt as the base of many desserts, cakes and other sweet treats.

Yogurt is an invaluable ingredient for so many sweet treats because it carries fruit flavours well, combines with many other ingredients and can offer lower fat alternatives to traditional choices.

Banana Smoothie

1 banana
1 cup Easiyo Passionfruit Yogurt
1 scoop vanilla ice cream
1 teaspoon honey
1 tablespoon wheatgerm

Peel banana. Chop roughly and place in a blender or processor. Add yogurt, ice cream, honey and wheatgerm and blend or process until smooth and creamy. Serve immediately.

Serves 1.

Strawberry Daiquiri

Serve this as a summer aperitif or as an end to an alfresco luncheon.

1 cup fresh or frozen strawberries
1 cup Easiyo Strawberry Yogurt
½ cup white rum
About 6 ice-cubes

Hull strawberries if using fresh. Place in a food processor or blender with yogurt and rum and blend or process until smooth. With motor running, add ice-cubes one at a time and process until ice-cubes are crushed.

Serves 2.

Orange Julius

Squeeze your own juice for this or use a ready-prepared variety. Adding the ice-cubes with the motor running stops them jamming the blade.

2 cups freshly squeezed orange juice
2 cups Easiyo Natural or Apricot Yogurt

Freeze orange juice in ice-cube trays. Place 1 cup of yogurt in a blender or food processor. Turn motor on and add half the ice-cubes. Blend or process until ice-cubes are ground. Repeat with remaining mixture. Serve immediately.

Serves 3 to 4.

Banana Smoothie, Strawberry Daiquiri, Orange Julius

Jungle Nectar

A blender makes a smoother drink than a food processor. If you have a choice, choose the blender.

1 banana

227g can crushed pineapple in juice

1 kiwifruit

1 cup chopped fresh or canned drained apricots

1 cup ice-cubes

1 cup Easiyo Natural Yogurt

Peel banana and chop roughly. Place in a blender or food processor. Add undrained pineapple. Peel kiwifruit and chop roughly. Add to processor with apricots. Blend or process until combined. With motor running, add ice-cubes one at a time then pour in yogurt and blend or process until smooth and creamy. Serve immediately.

Serves 4.

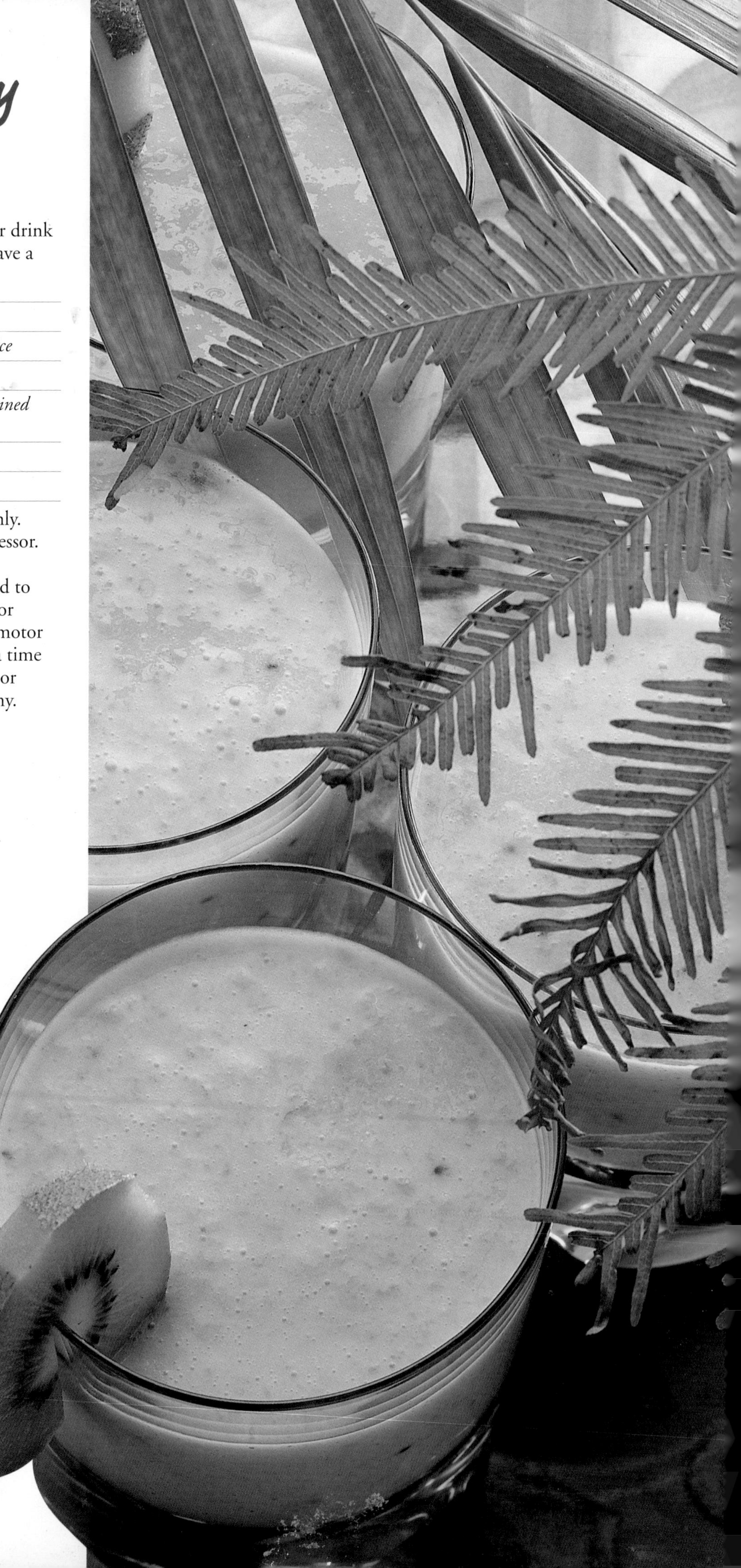

Jungle Nectar

Apricot Brownie

Use this as a dessert if wished by serving with apricot yogurt sauce or use as something to have in your cake tins.

1 cup chopped dried apricots
1 cup Easiyo Natural Yogurt
200g butter
1 cup brown sugar
3 eggs
1 teaspoon vanilla essence
1 1/4 cups flour
2 teaspoons baking powder
Icing sugar

Mix apricots and yogurt together and set aside while preparing remaining ingredients. Melt butter in a saucepan large enough to mix all the ingredients. Remove from heat and mix in brown sugar. Add eggs and beat with a wooden spoon until combined. Add vanilla and apricot yogurt mixture. Sift flour and baking powder into mixture and beat until combined. Line a 18 x 27cm sponge roll tin with baking paper. Pour mixture into this and bake at 180°C for 40 minutes or until brownie springs back when lightly touched. Dust with icing sugar. If serving as a dessert, cut into 8 pieces and serve warm with Apricot Yogurt Sauce.

Serves 8.

APRICOT YOGURT SAUCE

1 cup dried apricots
1 cup apricot nectar
1 cup Easiyo Natural Yogurt

Place apricots and nectar in a saucepan and cook over a medium heat for 10 minutes. Puree in a blender or food processor. Fold through yogurt, leaving partly mixed to give a swirl effect if wished.

Makes 1 1/2 cups.

Apricot Brownie

Date and Orange Muffins

2 cups flour

3 teaspoons baking powder

¼ cup sugar

1 cup chopped stoned dates

50g butter

2 eggs

1 teaspoon grated orange rind

¼ cup orange juice

1½ cups Easiyo Natural Yogurt

Sift flour and baking powder into a bowl. Mix in sugar and dates. Make a well in the centre of the dry ingredients. Melt butter. Lightly beat eggs, orange rind and juice together. Pour butter, egg mixture and yogurt into the well in the dry ingredients and mix until just combined. Three-quarters fill greased muffin tins with the mixture. Bake at 200°C for 15 minutes or until muffins spring back when lightly touched.

Makes about 12.

Wholemeal and Yogurt Scones

1 cup flour

1 cup wholemeal flour

3 teaspoons baking powder

½ teaspoon salt

1 cup Easiyo Apricot Yogurt

50g butter

¼ cup water

Milk to glaze

Sift flours, baking powder and salt into a bowl, returning husks from the sieve to the flours in bowl. Make a well in the centre of dry ingredients. Add yogurt to dry ingredients. Melt butter. Add butter and water to bowl and mix quickly to a soft dough with a knife. Transfer mixture to a lightly floured surface and knead lightly. Roll or pat dough out to a 3.5cm thickness. Using a 6cm scone cutter, cut out rounds. Place on an oven tray. Brush tops lightly with milk. Bake at 200°C for 20 minutes or until golden.

Makes about 8.

Lemon Curd Ice Cream Terrine

1 cup lemon curd

1 cup Easiyo Natural Yogurt

250g pot sour cream

FILLING

1 cup Easiyo Passionfruit or Apricot Yogurt

1/4 cup orange marmalade

Mix lemon curd, yogurt and sour cream together. Pour half the mixture into a 25 x 10cm loaf tin and freeze until firm. Spread filling over. Freeze until firm. Top with remaining lemon mixture and freeze until ready to serve. Remove terrine from tin. Cut into slices to serve.

FILLING

Mix yogurt and marmalade together until combined.

Serves 8 to 10.

Nothing Like Boarding School Rice Pud

In days gone by, rice pud was cooked under the Sunday roast. It has memories of disgust for some but great pleasures for others. My childhood memories are of disgust but, as tastes evolve, this rice pud version is wonderful.

2 eggs

2 tablespoons brown sugar

2 1/2 cups Easiyo Natural Yogurt

1/2 teaspoon vanilla essence

1/4 cup short grain rice

1 cup Easiyo Raspberry Yogurt Flavouring

Ground nutmeg

Lightly beat eggs and sugar until combined. Mix in yogurt and vanilla. Sprinkle rice into a 6 cup capacity ovenproof dish. Pour over raspberry flavouring then pour over yogurt mixture. Bake at 160°C for 1 1/2 hours. Dust with nutmeg to serve.

Serves 4.

Honey and Pistachio Nut Roulade

4 eggs

½ cup sugar

2 tablespoons honey

1 cup flour

2 teaspoons baking powder

FILLING

150ml cream

1 cup Easiyo Natural Yogurt

½ cup chopped roasted pistachio nuts

1 tablespoon honey

Separate eggs. Beat egg whites until stiff. Gradually add sugar, beating well until egg whites are stiff and glossy. Fold in egg yolks and honey. Sift flour and baking powder into egg mixture. Line a 20 x 30cm sponge roll tin with baking paper. Spoon mixture into prepared tin. Smooth the surface with a palate knife. Bake at 200°C for 10 to 15 minutes or until roulade springs back when lightly touched. Turn onto a clean piece of baking paper dusted with icing sugar. Remove baking paper from bottom of roulade and roll up from the short side. Leave to cool. When cold, unroll and remove paper. Spread with filling and re-roll. Place seam-side down on a serving plate. Cut into slices and serve.

FILLING

Whip cream until it holds its shape. Fold in yogurt, nuts and honey.

Serves 4 to 6.

Lemon Curd Ice Cream Terrine, Nothing Like Boarding School Rice Pud, Honey and Pistachio Nut Roulade

Quick'n'Easy

Honey Yogurt Flan

400g packet sweet short pasty
Icing sugar
FILLING
2 cups Easiyo Natural Yogurt
½ cup sugar
½ cup honey
1 tablespoons lemon juice
2 teaspoons grated lemon rind
3 eggs

Roll pastry out to fit a 25cm flan tin or dish. Trim to fit. Prick base with a fork and bake at 190°C for 10 to 15 minutes or until pastry looks cooked but not golden. Leave to cool. Pour in filling. Bake at 160°C for 45 to 50 minutes or until set. Dust with icing sugar and serve either hot or at room temperature.

FILLING

Mix yogurt, sugar, honey, lemon juice, rind and eggs together until combined.

Serves 6 to 8.

Special Whipped Cream

This cream is particularly good with berries as the sharp taste the yogurt gives it really complements the berry flavours.

300ml cream
1 cup Easiyo Natural Yogurt

Whip cream until thick. Fold in yogurt.

Makes 2½ cups.

Honey Yogurt Flan, Honey Gingerbread, French Apple Crisp

Honey Gingerbread

It breaks my time-saving heart to see people grease the sides of a tin they line with baking paper. You don't need to and it defeats the purpose of using baking paper if you do.

100g butter

¾ cup brown sugar

¼ cup honey

½ cup Easiyo Natural Yogurt

1 teaspoon baking soda

2 eggs

2½ cups flour

2 tablespoons ground ginger

Melt butter, brown sugar and honey together in a saucepan large enough to mix all the ingredients. Cool slightly. Mix yogurt and baking soda together. Beat eggs into batter mixture, sift in flour and ginger, and fold in with yogurt mixture. Line the bottom of a 20 x 12cm tin and spoon the mixture in. Bake at 180°C for 30 to 35 minutes or until gingerbread springs back when lightly touched. Cool in tin for 10 minutes before turning onto a cooling rack. Serve with butter if wished.

French Apple Crisp

400g can solid pack apples

2 eggs

1½ cups Easiyo Berry Fruits Yogurt

2 tablespoons sugar

½ teaspoon ground cloves

TOPPING

1 cup rolled oats

½ cup flour

½ cup brown sugar

50g butter

¼ cup Easiyo Natural Yogurt

Spread apples in the base of a 30 x 18cm oval ovenproof dish. Lightly beat eggs, yogurt, sugar and cloves together. Pour over apples. Sprinkle over topping. Bake at 180°C for 35 to 45 minutes or until mixture is set and topping golden.

TOPPING

Mix rolled oats, flour and sugar together. Melt butter and mix through oat mixture with yogurt. Mix until combined.

Serves 4

Quick'n'Easy

Fashionable Semolina Cake

150g butter
1 cup sugar
1 teaspoon vanilla
4 eggs
1 teaspoon grated orange rind
2 cups semolina
1 teaspoon baking powder
1 teaspoon baking soda
1 cup Easiyo Natural Yogurt
SYRUP
1 cup sugar
½ cup water
2 tablespoons lemon juice
1 tablespoon honey

Melt butter in a saucepan large enough to mix all the ingredients. Add sugar and stir until dissolved. Remove from heat and cool slightly. Mix in vanilla, eggs and orange rind, mixing until combined. Mix semolina, baking powder and baking soda together and fold into butter mixture with yogurt. Line a 20 x 30cm sponge roll tin with baking paper and spoon mixture into this. Bake at 180°C for 25 to 30 minutes. Remove from oven and spoon syrup over. Serve warm with whipped cream as a dessert cake.

SYRUP

Mix sugar, water, lemon juice and honey together in a saucepan. Heat gently until completely combined. Set aside while preparing remaining ingredients.

Serves 8.

Fashionable Semolina Cake, Rob's Cut-and-Come-Again Fruit Cake, Lemon Yogurt Nut Cake

Rob's Cut-and-Come-Again Fruit Cake

A friend of mine makes this style of fruit cake once a week for her husband's lunch box. After more than 20 years I would have expected him to have tired of it, so I hope this cake will be a change of flavour for him. Use flour suitable for fruit cakes for this recipe.

2 cups mixed fruit
125g butter
3/4 cup brown sugar
1 1/2 teaspoons mixed spice
1/2 cup orange juice
2 eggs
1/2 cup Easiyo Passionfruit Yogurt
2 cups flour
3 teaspoons baking powder

Mix fruit, butter, sugar, spice and orange juice together in a pan. Bring to the boil, reduce heat and simmer for 5 minutes. Remove from heat and cool slightly so adding the eggs does not scramble them. Add eggs, yogurt, flour and baking powder and beat with a wooden spoon until combined. Line the bottom of a 20cm round cake tin with baking paper. Bake at 160°C for 1 1/2 hours or until an inserted skewer comes out clean. Cool in tin for 10 minutes before turning onto a cooling rack.

Lemon Yogurt Nut Cake

Don't switch off from making this cake because it uses six eggs. Compare the cost of eggs with half a pack of butter (which this recipe doesn't, but could, use). Now that puts it in perspective doesn't it? Have eggs at room temperature for a better result.

6 eggs
1/2 cup sugar
1 1/4 cups Easiyo Natural Yogurt
1/4 cup olive oil
1 1/2 cups flour
2 teaspoons baking powder
2 cups mixed fresh roasted nuts such as pecans, almonds and shelled pistachio nuts
1 tablespoon grated lemon rind
TOPPING
1 cup chopped mixed roasted nuts
1/4 cup raw sugar

Separate eggs. Beat egg yolks with half the sugar until pale and creamy. Fold in yogurt and oil. Beat egg whites until stiff. Beat in remaining sugar and beat until thick and glossy. Fold in flour, baking powder and nuts. Fold egg white mixture through egg yolk mixture with lemon rind. Line a 20cm round cake tin with baking paper. Spoon mixture into prepared tin and bake at 180°C for 30 minutes. Remove from oven. Press over topping and continue to bake for a further 25 to 30 minutes or until cake is cooked and springs back when lightly touched. Serve warm with whipped cream mixed with yogurt.

TOPPING

Mix nuts and sugar together.

Serves 6 to 8.

Quick 'n' Easy

INDEX

Dips and Nibbles

Dressings & Marinades

Curries

Light Meals

Main Courses

Sweet Treats